745.4

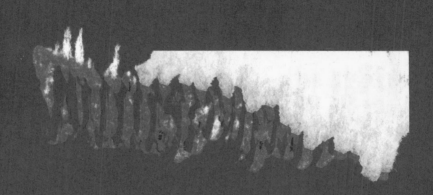

STUDIES IN
DESIGN

STUDIES IN
DESIGN

DR. CHRISTOPHER DRESSER

STUDIO EDITIONS
LONDON

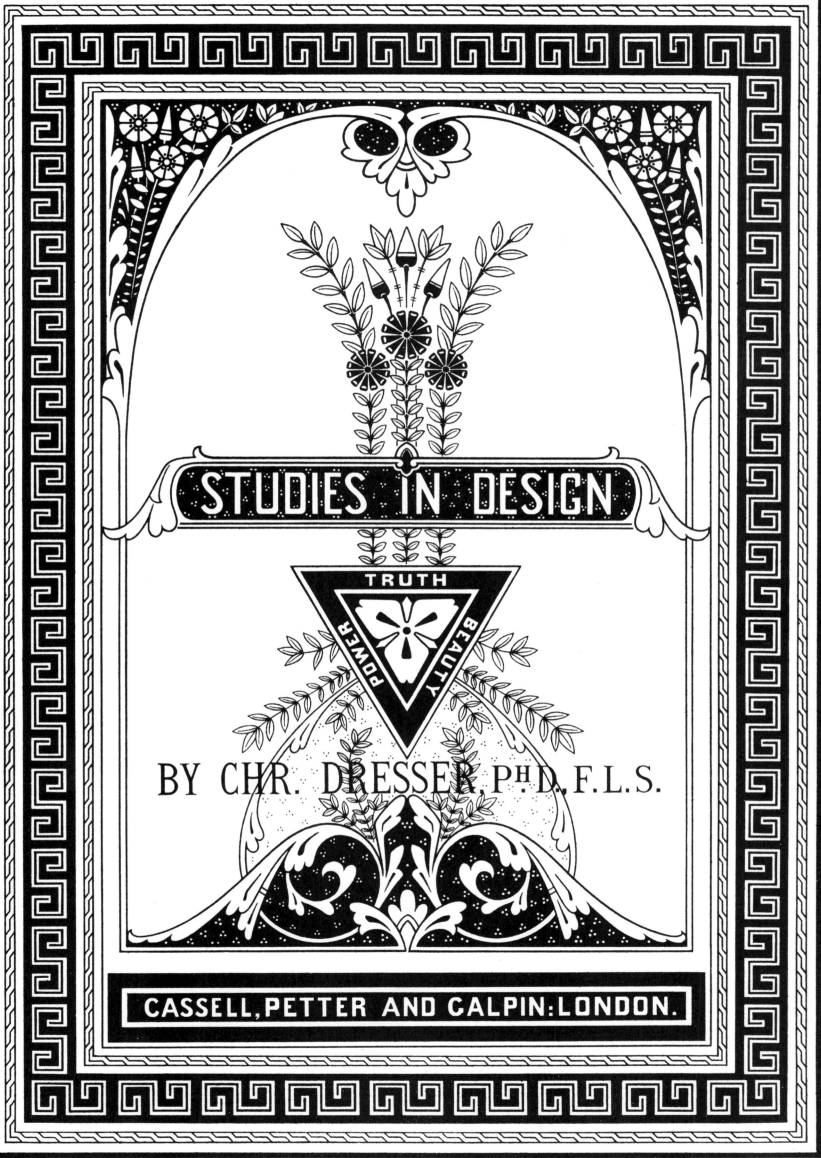

STUDIES IN DESIGN

TRUTH

POWER

BEAUTY

BY CHR. DRESSER, PʰD, F.L.S.

CASSELL, PETTER AND GALPIN: LONDON.

Dʀ. DRESSER, INV.

A. GOATER LITHO NOTTM.

Studies in Design was originally published in 1876
by Cassell, Petter and Galpin, London

This edition published by Studio Editions,
a division of Bestseller Publications Ltd,
Princess House, 50 Eastcastle Street,
London W1N 7AP in 1988

Copyright © Studio Editions, 1988

ISBN 1 85170 174 5

Printed and bound in Hong Kong

INTRODUCTION

In a era obsessed with design and the expression of taste as revealed in the choice of consumer goods, Dr. Christopher Dresser would seem to strike an intriguingly contemporary note. Hailed as a pioneer of the modern movement, his theories have proved consistently attractive to historians of design and yet, in the complexity and self-made strength of his character and in his confident use of maxims such as 'Knowledge is Power', he remains essentially as typical a figure of the nineteenth century as Samuel Smiles. In order properly to understand his crucial contribution, it is, therefore, important to view his theories and achievements in the context of the artistic and scientific milieu in which he formed his ideas.

Dresser's world was that of the, then, newly formed Government Schools of Design, the intellectual cutting-edge of the Department of Science and Art and the forcing ground of new thinking concerning the interrelationship of the arts and sciences and the benefits to be derived from the application of the principles of taste and design to the manufacturing industries. This world was dominated by the theories and teaching of a powerful circle of artists and educationalists, design-reformers and a new breed of art administrators including Richard Redgrave, Owen Jones and Sir Henry Cole, the prime mover of the Great Exhibition of 1851 and the first Director of the South Kensington Museum. Dresser came under the influence of these formidable men, the arbiters of advanced taste in England, during his formative years at the Schools between 1847 and 1854. There he developed the dual interests in botany and design which were to form the basis of all his subsequent work as a lecturer, writer and practising designer.

Dresser's contribution to pure botanical studies was not without importance and earned him the Doctorate from the University of Jena of which he was so proud, but his great reputation now rests upon series of papers, treatises and beautifully printed pattern-books of the 1860s and 70s in which he expounded his innovative theories concerning the application of the principles of form and colour to be discovered in Nature to pattern making and ornamental design. As early as 1856 Dresser had contributed a plate of conventionalized flower motifs to Owen Jones's *Grammar of Ornament*, but his first major independent work was the synthesis of art and botany, *The Art of Decorative Design* of 1862, the book which firmly established his standing. From this date Dresser concentrated on freelance design for all manner of manufacturing industries, designing crucially innovative domestic metalware and furnishings and at the same time developing the interests in interior decoration which were to absorb his later years.

The present volume, *Studies in Design* which was published between 1874 and 1876 with, as Dresser pointed out, 'the hope of assisting to bring about a better style of decoration for our houses' reflects not only the strength of his pattern designing based on angular, stylized plant forms and other geometric motifs, but also reveals a new, rich and sombre palette of colours eminently suitable for the decoration of the rooms of the day. For this reason the volume became a bible for the decorators of the Aesthetic Movement and has remained to this day a classic in the genre of design books.

STEPHEN CALLOWAY
VICTORIA AND ALBERT MUSEUM,
LONDON

PREFACE.

———◦◦◦———

I HAVE prepared this Work with the hope of assisting to bring about a better style of decoration for our houses. My book is intended to help the decorator and to enable those who live in decorated houses to judge, to an extent, of the merit of the ornament around them. It will also, it is hoped, aid the designer and the manufacturer of decorated objects, by suggesting to them useful ideas.

Tower Cressy, Notting Hill,
　　London.

STUDIES IN DESIGN.

CHAPTER I.

INTRODUCTORY.

A WEALTHY community always erects decorated buildings. In the progressive advancement of a civilised nation, first come industries, and then the fine arts. Cain was a tiller of the ground, and Abel was a keeper of sheep, but Jubal was the father of all such as handle the harp and the organ; and Tubal-cain was an instructor of every artificer in brass and iron. The fine arts flourish when necessities are supplied. The wealthy decorate their houses; but if the necessities of existence are not satisfied, decorations are not called for. Decoration is a luxury; it is something superadded to what is necessary. Yet the desire for decoration is natural to the human mind. Savages tattoo or ornament their bodies, and array themselves in what they regard as decorative objects; and even the instruments with which they surround themselves —their spears and their bows—are ornamented; but savage communities devote no time to husbandry—they live simply by the chase,—hence the innate desire for ornament manifests itself even when man is in a barbaric condition. Princes and merchants decorate their houses, and, even as savages, have their surroundings of decorative character.

That England has become a rich country no one doubts. As a result, houses are being decorated in every part of the kingdom; but knowledge of the immutable laws of ornamentation are necessary to those who would decorate wisely and well. I have seen many decorated houses, so called, that are less satisfactory than if each room had been simply whitewashed, for they are offensive, while white walls would at least look wholesome.

Decorations, to be satisfying to the educated, must manifest knowledge. The caprices of the decorator can only afford pleasure when they reveal knowledge, and the decorator should have wisdom as well as knowledge; for unless the decoration is done wisely as well as with understanding, it may yet fail to please those who are best able to appreciate good ornament.

No man should be censured for his ignorance if he has had no opportunity of acquiring knowledge. Few are altogether without the means of gaining learning; and much may be done by the diligent, even if opportunities are both rare and poor. He who has learned to think has learned much, but the greatest thinker may learn from the contemplation of what others have done. I submit my present work to those who desire to decorate houses in a manner that shall reveal their knowledge; but it will be most useful to that man who can use my ideas as grades to his own thought, and who can cull from my examples whatever is right and true, and, by digestion in his own mind, give to my forms new features and individuality of expression, throwing aside all that is not concordant with his own feelings of what is true and what is right.

The sketches published in this volume are my original designs, with the exception of one or two examples, which are by my advanced students and assistants. They are in all cases expressions of my individual feeling. They have been prepared during the last fifteen years, and many of them have been drawn during my best and happiest moments.

As newness of idea must be sought after as well as refinement of expression, I have to beg the indulgent criticism of those who seek fresh ideas in this work; for the efforts at realising what is new must ever be attended with the danger of being extravagant and the risk of being eccentric. I have striven to attain newness, and my sketches go forth to the world. I beg lenient consideration.

CHAPTER II.

ON THE PRODUCTION OF ORNAMENT.

I THINK it but right that I reveal in this chapter the conditions under which many of my designs for ornamental decorations have been produced.

Having knowledge of the art of drawing, and possessing that power over the vehicles with which I delineate objects, or express thoughts in forms, which enables me to make shapes at discretion without even the slightest expenditure of thought on the means whereby the ideas, or forms, are expressed, I sit down to design a pattern—say for a carpet, a wall decoration, a damask hanging, or whatever I desire to ornament. I am never at a loss for an idea; but when in ordinary mood, I appeal to scholarship—to knowledge of what has been done, rather than to any faculty by which distinct originality is evolved; and from my knowledge I arrange or produce a pattern. I may settle that the pattern is to be Arabian, Chinese, Indian, or Moresque in style, and decide to produce Arabian, Chinese, Indian, or Moresque ornament. Knowing what the Arabians, Chinese, Indians, and Moors have for centuries produced when they have ornamented a fabric, or surface, such as I desire to decorate, I commence to produce forms similar to those employed by the particular people that I elect to follow, and thus I produce an Arabian, or Chinese, or Indian, or Moresque pattern. But my success in the production of such a pattern depends largely upon the extent to which I become, in feeling, for the time a Chinaman, or Arabian, or such as the case requires. But I must not only become, in spirit, a citizen of the country whose ornament I wish to simulate, but I must become, in a sense, a scholar of that country. He who is ignorant cannot express in his works a knowledge which he does not possess. The learned alone can express by their works learning. In order that I enter into the spirit of the Oriental, I often find it necessary to inform myself of the religion, mode of government, climate, and habits of a people; for it is only by understanding their faith and usages that I can comprehend the spirit of their ornament, and become for a time one of them in feeling. Being familiar with the ornamental forms employed by a particular people, and being acquainted with their religious faith, mode of government, social arrangements, the nature of their food, and the character of their climate, I can, by allowing the mind to absorb foreign feelings till it is pervaded by them, so far become for the time a foreigner in spirit that I can produce ornament having much of the spirit of that which I have decided to simulate, and which may even be indistinguishable from native work. Under such feelings and circumstances, the Arabian borderings forming Plate XXIX. were produced.

But the influence to which I would call special attention is more nearly allied to inspiration, and is that which the diligent and advanced student alone experiences. At times every true artist is the subject of peculiar yet, unfortunately, transient power, which for the time renders him superior to his common self. These are the moments that the student must never lose—moments in which he knows no law, and in which he appears to be raised above the necessity of appealing to scholastic learning. It is at these moments that Genius comes to his aid and guides his hand. But be assured that this aid is only given to those who by industry and patient toil acquire that knowledge which makes them, to speak figuratively, fit companions of the Muses.

These happy moments are not always present with us, and yet we have to design ornaments which lend beauty to what they invest. I cannot too strongly urge upon the ornamentist the necessity for ever seeking new ideas, and for training the mind to see new forms, or combinations of shapes, in everything that the eye can rest upon. Sometimes mere straws in the street may suggest good ornaments, and a bent reed reflected in a lake may furnish a fresh thought for a decorative composition. Even things with which we are familiar may at a particular time present themselves in a new aspect, and thus furnish an idea which may be of value: thus about eighteen years since I made sketches of the frost which we commonly see on the windows of our rooms in winter; but it was eight years later that I perceived in these sketches a new style of ornament,—hence we have Plates XIX. and XXXIV.

The sense of humour finds expression in grotesque forms. Plates II., VI., VII., and XIV. are illustrations.

CHAPTER III.

ON THE NECESSITY FOR GAINING POWER OF DRAWING AND KNOWLEDGE OF THE PRINCIPLES
OF ORNAMENT AT THE SAME TIME.

WHAT I have said in my last chapter shows with sufficient clearness that no one can become an ornamentist who has not perfect mastery over the pencil.   I will not say that it is impossible for a man who cannot draw almost perfectly to produce an ornament with some merits ; but this I do assert, that unless the power exercised by an individual over the pencil has become as great as the power which is exerted over the pen by a ready writer, he cannot become an ornamentist in the higher and true sense of the term.   So long as he has to think of the means by which the end is attained, the whole energy of the mind is not directed towards the realisation of his mental conception, for part of the brain-force is expended upon the means by which the idea is being realised in form.

Let it not be supposed that I wish a power of drawing to be learned by sketching objects merely for the sake of sketching, for this is a general and grievous mistake made in the teaching of drawing.   It is possible to learn the special features and peculiar qualities of all styles of ornament while learning to draw ; and it is as easy to draw forms which will give knowledge of historic ornament as it is to draw objects which are calculated to give practice in drawing only, and which afford no knowledge that assists at the same time in the training of the mind and the hand.   Let the student take the flower of the lotus, or blue water-lily (*Nymphœa cœrulea*), which is to be seen in the water-tanks in Kew Gardens, the Crystal Palace, Sydenham, and other places, and draw it.   This is the "lotus" of the ancient Egyptians, and is one of their sacred flowers ;* after drawing the flower and re-drawing it till you can delineate it with delicacy, feeling, and refinement, and have got sketches of it as a bud, as an expanded blossom, and in every intermediate stage, commence to consider and copy this flower as portrayed by the Egyptians.   On almost every mummy-case it appears many times, and every work on Egyptian ornament gives it.   If, together with practice of drawing, you acquire knowledge of the manner in which this flower was used in ornament, and read up what is known of its symbolic significance, you have at the same time been learning to draw

---

* I have spoken somewhat fully of this flower, and how it became sacred, in my " Principles of Decorative Design."

(and a special interest is given to the acquisition of this power), gathering knowledge of the manner in which a flower has been used as an ornament by a people who were great ornamentists, and have been learning the symbolic significance of a characteristic historic ornament.

In like manner the sacred bean (*Nelumbrium speciosum*) of China, India, and Japan should be drawn, and then the various forms which it assumes in Chinese, Japanese, and Indian ornaments should be traced out.

The common passion flower (*Passiflora cærulea*) should also be copied, and its modifications of form as a mediæval ornament noted: its symbolism should also be learned. Thus the Passion of our Lord is set forth by this flower, in the centre of which are the three nails radiating from the top of the round-headed hammer. Below the head of the hammer protrude five yellow members—the five wounds; at the base of the hammer is the crown of thorns, and spreading from this are glory-rays. There are then ten flower-leaves—the Apostles, Peter being absent because of the denial, and Judas because of the betrayal of Christ. At the back of the flower are three leaves—the Holy Trinity; the green leaves on the stems are five-lobed—the hand with the five fingers of the betrayer; then there are the tendrils —the cords with which Christ was bound. Such is the symbolism of this strange flower.

I would also advise the learner to take one or two small portions of Alhambraic ornament, then one or two small portions of Arabian ornament, then of Turkish, then of Persian; and while drawing these forms, which are not symbolic, notice carefully the resemblances and differences between the ornaments belonging to these various styles, and thus make himself master of the characteristic qualities of each.

In concluding my remarks about drawing, I must call attention to the fact that, to the artist, the term "drawing" means much more than it does to the general reader. We frequently hear the remark made in respect to a great painter, that "he cannot draw," and yet his pictures are sought after and have great merits. Here it is not pretended that the man cannot draw at all; but it is meant simply that in drawing qualities he lacks that exquisite subtlety of execution—that power of expressing with exact forms the knowledge of refinement of shape, and delicacy of line, which some men have. He may be a great colourist, or excel at composition, and yet lack the highest drawing power. Strive after the expression of exquisite delicacy of feeling and subtlety of perception in every shape that you make.*

* The student will do well to study native Japanese drawings of flowers (Japanese books can now be got at many fancy warehouses); and he will do well to look carefully at "The Preacher," by Owen Jones, especially at that page near the middle of the book, where the central strip of ornament is blue, and the words commence with "Who knoweth the spirit of man?"

CHAPTER IV.

ON THE NECESSITY FOR KNOWLEDGE OF HISTORIC ORNAMENT.

No one, however original in thought he may be, and however subtle in his perception of beauty, can become a great ornamentist unless he has knowledge of what has been done by those who have worked at his art under various influences and at various times.   Palissy, the potter, who rediscovered the glaze of earthenware, boasted that he had never seen a book ; but his works are as useless and stupid as can well be imagined.   A dish with snails, toads, and lizards in relief upon it, is not a thing of utility ; and however well modelled the reptiles and molluscs may be, there is such a want of beauty in the Palissy works that as mere ornaments they are most unsatisfactory.   The genius of Palissy, if combined with knowledge and guided by wisdom, would certainly have led to the production of works which would have been valued for their art worth, and not merely as curious objects.

Before the ornamentist can produce work of the highest character—work by which a maximum of knowledge and learning are revealed—he must have understanding of Egyptian, Greek, Persian, Arabian, Indian, Chinese, Japanese, and Mediæval ornament at least ; and to this should be added an acquaintance with Roman and Italian decorations, although so much that is false is mingled with the good in these two last styles, that the advanced student should alone study them. It is not sufficient that we know the forms used by the peoples of these various countries, and the manner in which they combined these shapes ; we must also know the spirit which actuated the designer when producing his work.

The Egyptians were great slave-owners, and they were hard masters.   There was severity in their every act.   Yet with the rulers there was also dignity and nobleness. In all their ornament you will find these characters manifested—the very characteristics necessary to the greatness of a nation at that period of the world's history. But besides the dignity and severity of the drawing of the Egyptians, almost every form was the symbol of a special thought or idea.   The people could not read, and to an unlettered people, forms, used as symbols, have often successfully appealed.   The significance of these symbols should be understood by all who wish to comprehend Egyptian ornament.   Greek ornament was only intended as an expression of the most perfect refinement of form, and of knowledge of natural laws; but as I have entered into this subject more fully in my " Principles of Decorative Design" than I can do here, it is unnecessary that I reiterate what I have already said.

Egyptian ornament, being symbolic, is not suited to our wants. Yet the severity and dignity of the drawing we may well copy, for they are noble qualities, and are our just inheritance.

This single remark will show that a value attaches to the study of historic ornament. We gather from the various styles those broad and general qualities which are applicable in all time and under all circumstances.

During our study of past ornament we find, however, much which it is perhaps wise to discard, and much which we must set aside emphatically; for qualities become apparent which are base and wrong, as well as those which are excellent. We also meet with many forms and combinations of shapes which, while useful ornaments to the people who created them, are unfitted to our purposes, as they reveal what we regard as a superstition, a folly, or that which has in our eyes an evil tendency. But with what is to us useless there is combined much that is noble and beautiful, and in most of the great "styles" of ornament we discover numerous truths which are suited to all times and to all requirements. Study, I say, whatever has gone before; not with the view of becoming a copyist, but with the object of gaining knowledge, and of seeking out general truths and broad principles which will serve you as they have served the noble and the good in times long past. The passions, feelings, and aspirations of men in this day are similar to those of men who lived three thousand years ago; and with a like amount of knowledge, and similar surroundings, man would now do much as he did then. Whatever is common to all time and is noble in its tendency belongs to us by right; and we who live in these later days should learn from the experience of those who have gone before; and our works should be superior to those of our ancestors, inasmuch as we can look back upon a longer experience than they could.

CHAPTER V.

ON THE POWER OF ART TO ENNOBLE AND BEAUTIFY, AND ON MEANS TO BE EMPLOYED.

BEFORE we commence considering the manner in which ornament should be applied to rooms, it is desirable that we notice the purpose and aim of the true decorator. If of plain form and soft colour, the walls of an apartment are sure not to be offensive; in a sense they are satisfying; but if a true artist commences work on these walls he will, by his art, give to them a charm which they could not possess if art were not applied to them. By the agency of true art we can give to an apartment an amount of beauty which it could not possess without it. By the application of art, a very barn may become a palace. The powers of art are equal to the achievement of almost any amount of exaltation of a room, fabric, domestic utensil, or whatever it is applied to.

Art can lend to an apartment not only beauty, but such refinement as will cause it to have an elevating influence on those who dwell in it. But in order to this the decorator must be refined. If the well is bitter, the water flowing from it will be bitter; if sweet, it will give forth sweet waters. No decorator who is coarse and vulgar in thought and perception can produce works which will have a refining influence on others. For the decorations to be pure, the mind from which they flow must be pure also.

If the decoration of an apartment is to be of the highest character, it must reveal a maximum amount of knowledge, of wisdom, and of purity on the part of its producer. If a man has knowledge, it is revealed by his words, his actions, his writings, his works. If he has wisdom, it shows itself in the manner in which he sets forth his knowledge. If he has refinement, it is manifested by his acts, and by every form that he draws. To the ignorant such manifestations may not be apparent, but by the educated they are always perceived. Can the ploughboy discern how a message passes along the electric wire? Can the street Arab decipher Egyptian hieroglyphics? For the ignorant we have no concern; to the educated who are possessed of knowledge and refinement we must appeal, and the opinions of such we alone regard.

Discouragement is often felt at work not being appreciated, I know; but it is easy to bear discouragement when there is the inward consciousness that it arises from the ignorance of the beholder. But there must be the full assurance of superior knowledge, and not merely the hope that the taste of the producer is in advance of that of the spectator. A man may possess true humility, and yet be fully conscious that he knows more than others. If, however, the occupant of an apartment fails to appreciate decorations because they are in advance of his taste and knowledge, he will yet learn to appreciate and value them if he but grow in knowledge. Besides this, there is a something about superior works which, though indescribable, seems to carry with them a conviction of their worth. However much the ignorant may sneer at that which is in advance of their powers of appreciation, they yet feel an inward consciousness of their own inability to judge of merit. If we do what we know to be good work—work full of knowledge, of beauty, of truth, and of power—we can rest satisfied, for all whose praise we covet will appreciate the value of what we do.

I have seen many a room called decorated which has been infinitely less desirable as an apartment than if it had been simply whitewashed. To decorate is to beautify. The mere addition of colours, or of colours and forms, to walls and to ceilings, does not necessarily render them beautiful. Only quite recently I entered an apartment with large windows, and through the windows was a lovely landscape diversified with hill and dale and richly-wooded slopes, and the walls of this room were of emerald green. Of all colours that could be chosen for the walls of such an apartment, this green was the worst. The soft tints of nature were altogether destroyed by the glaring colour of the walls ; and instead of what was without rendering the room more comfortable in appearance, and the colour of the walls rendering the landscape more attractive, all was confusion and want of harmony, and each made the other look offensive.

The attainment of repose is the highest aim of art. Repose cannot be found if forms are apparent which betoken ignorance, vulgarity, or coarseness. The eye will rest on a surface which reveals beauties of form, harmonies of colour, knowledge on the part of the decorator, and which has an absence of crude and garish qualities, and it will there find repose. Repose and harmony are art qualities ; glitter and attractiveness if largely indulged in are vulgarities. Yet how many rooms do we see in which every object is attractive and " loud," and yet between the various parts of the whole there is no harmony ? If we seek repose and refinement we are unlikely to fail in the discovery of what is true and noble.

CHAPTER VI.

ON THE MEANS BY WHICH REPOSE IS ATTAINABLE IN DECORATION.

IN my last chapter I insisted on the necessity for our achieving " repose " in all our decorations, as repose is an indispensable art quality; but the means by which repose was to be attained was not clearly set forth.

In the absence of a manifestation of knowledge, and in the absence of harmony, there cannot be repose; but it does not follow that the reverse must be true, and that because knowledge and harmony are revealed in our works, that there must necessarily be the sense of repose. There is such a thing as a harmony of lights, of bright spots, of glitters, and all glitter is antagonistic to rest. In the manner of the combination of gems we often detect knowledge and harmony; but a room with its sides formed of glittering surfaces could scarcely yield repose, even were it formed of parts of such tints as produce, when combined, a true harmony.

Rooms having their walls largely formed of glazed tiles, or of varnished surfaces, are rarely satisfactory, for the reflections which they of necessity throw out are exciting, and excitement is antagonistic to rest. Excitement is endurable and even useful to the system, if sparingly indulged in ; but the constant endurance of excitement is exhausting.

But how are we to achieve the necessary amount of repose in our rooms? We need not paint the walls of our apartments grey, nor of mud-colour, neither need we make them black; indeed, the highest sense of repose—*i.e.*, dreamy, soothing repose, may be realised where the brightest colours are employed. Repose is attained by the absence of any want. A plain wall of dingy colour reveals a want; it does not then supply all that is necessary to the production of a sense of quiet and rest. A wall may be covered with the richest decoration, and yet be of such a character that the eye will rest upon it and be satisfied.

If strong colours are used upon walls and ceilings, it is usually desirable that they be employed in very small masses; thus blue, red, and yellow may be used upon a wall (the three primary colours), either alone, or together with white, gold, or black, and be so mingled that the general effect will be perfectly neutral, and an effect so produced may induce the highest sense of repose. There will, however, be a glow, or radiance, about such a wall; yet this radiance will only give richness to neutrality, and this is desirable.

Those effects which are "subtle"—which are not commonplace—which are attained by the expenditure of special skill or knowledge, are the best, provided that the end which is most desired is attained by them. A tertiary colour which is formed of two parts of yellow and one of red and one of blue—in fact, a citrine—is neutral. But a wall covered with a well-designed pattern of minute parts, with the separate members coloured red, blue, and yellow—the yellow being in relation to the blue and the red as two is to one *—would be neutral, yet it would be refined and glowing in effect, and thus it would exceed in merit the mere tertiary tint on the wall.

The white ceilings which we have in our rooms are almost fatal to the production of those qualities which yield the sense of repose or rest. A harmony between walls and a ceiling of cream tint † is much more easily attained than between walls and a white ceiling; but there is no reason whatever why a ceiling should not be blue, or any dark colour. No satisfactory room, of dark general aspect, can look well if the ceiling is white, and rooms which are somewhat dark in tone are often desirable. Furniture looks best on a dark ground, unless it be white and gold, when it is invariably execrable. Persons always look better against a somewhat dark background, and pictures on light strongly-figured walls are rarely sufficiently attractive to call to themselves the least attention. If it can be had, I like much window-space, to let in light, but the walls I prefer of darkish hue.

If the room is dark through lack of light, the walls may be light above, and have a dark dado—that is, the lower third, or any desired portion, may be dark, and the upper portion light. If this arrangement is adopted, and the upper part of the wall and the ceiling are each of cream tint, while in the cornice there is a rather broad line of deep blue, and one or more lines of pale blue, and perhaps a very fine line of red, these colours being all separated from each other by white—or, in the absence of a cornice, if the ceiling is surrounded by a border in blue and white—the effect will appear to be lighter and brighter than if the room were all white, and yet there will be a certain amount of repose about the general effect such as could not be easily attained were the ceiling white.

By our decorations we must ever seek to achieve repose, but we must always remember that repose is compatible with richness, subtlety, and radiance of effect.

---

* This is not rigidly correct, but for more exact information I must refer the reader to my "Principles of Decorative Design," pp. 40, 47, 48.

† A tint formed by the admixture of a small portion of middle-chrome—that chrome which is half-way between the colour of the lemon and of a deep-coloured orange—with white.

CHAPTER VII.

ON THE NECESSITY OF NEWNESS OF STYLE IN ORNAMENT.

I HAVE insisted upon the study of historic ornament as a necessary part of the education of an ornamentist, but I have not done so with the view of his being enabled thereby to produce works in imitation of the Greeks, the Indians, the Japanese, and other peoples, although it is always advantageous to have the power of producing ornaments in any required style. It is obvious that no past style of ornament is precisely suited to our wants : with the symbolism of the Egyptians we can have but little sympathy; Greek ornament, although without symbolic forms, is so intimately associated with a style of architecture which is only suited to a more genial climate than ours, that we can scarcely use it ; Indian ornament is too lavish to meet our general requirements; Alhambraic is too gorgeous ; and in all past styles there are qualities which render them in some way unsuited for general adoption by us.

The very fact that past styles were so perfectly adapted to meet the wants, and express the feelings, of peoples living in climates different from our own, and of dissimilar feelings and religions, would go far, of itself, to show that they could not be suited to our general requirements. Gothic ornament, although in one form it arose in our own country, and reached a wide development amongst us, was too intimately associated with the religion of the Middle Ages to be suitable for domestic purposes, and of mediæval house decoration we know but little. These considerations force upon us the necessity for striving after newness of style in ornament, and render it desirable that we, to an extent, devote ourselves to the search after novelty. If a house is of pure Italian architecture, its ornamentation must be Italian in spirit; if the house is architecturally Greek, then the ornament must be Greek. The great majority of our English houses are, however, of no style. A plain square house is no more Italian than it is Greek, Persian, or Moorish, and the great majority of our new villa residences, while often called Italian, have scarcely one Italian characteristic. Many of the Gothic villas (so called) are not Gothic, and with the exception of perhaps a pointed door, or a lancet window, they are without a single Gothic feature. To all houses of no style one class of decoration is as well suited as another, and it is a no greater violation of consistency to decorate the rooms of a square house in the Persian, Moorish, or Chinese style, than it is to employ upon them Italian ornaments.

The objection to this mode of procedure is this: We are so constituted that when we see an apartment decorated in a marked style of ornament, we at once look for corresponding architectural characters; and if these are absent, we experience a sense of disappointment. I have, however, seen some gorgeous rooms decorated in the Persian style, which have been so well managed that this want was not apparent, but great skill is necessary to the achievement of this all-sufficient repose. As a rule, we may safely conclude that ornament, with newness of character, is that which is best suited to houses without distinctive architectural features; hence I have given in this work a preponderance of sketches which cannot be regarded as of any known style.

In all attempts at the production of what is new, there is a danger of being extreme, eccentric, or unrefined. A mere caricaturing of certain qualities of even the best ornament is not satisfying. The new ornament may have the dignity of the Egyptian, the grace of the Greek, the richness of the Arabian, the intricacy of plot of the Moorish, and so on, and be acceptable. It must be vigorous, and yet grace must not be despised. Simple forms may be employed, but there must be richness of conception in the design. Let us join in a search after the new, but let us ever guard against the production of eccentricities rather than the formation of just ornaments.

CHAPTER VIII

ON THE APPLICATION OF ORNAMENT TO BUILDINGS OF VARIOUS ARCHITECTURAL STYLES.

IT is obvious to all that if a building has pure architectural features there should be a unity of style between the decorations and the building; and, indeed, between the furniture, hangings, carpets, and whatever the house contains, and the architecture. If a house is truly Italian, its decorations should consist of Italian ornaments; if it is Greek, the decorations should be of Greek ornament; and if Gothic, the ornaments should be Gothic.

But these terms are broad. All styles of architecture and ornament have undergone modifications. The earliest Egyptian works are the best. Greek art probably attained its highest development when the Parthenon was built at Athens. Early Gothic—that of the thirteenth century—is superior to that of any later date. When we use the term Gothic, as applied to architecture, little but the use of the pointed arch is signified, so broad is the term; and when we speak of the Greek or Italian styles, we employ terms which are scarcely more definite.

I am considered by some rather heterodox in the views which I am now about to put forth, but I do not feel the necessity of confining myself, when designing in any particular style, to the production of only such forms, and such combinations of forms, as were used by the particular people whose decorations I wish to simulate. If I do so I am no longer a designer—a creator of ornaments—for I become a mere copyist. What I do, when wishing to design in any particular style, is this: I study the style in all its modifications, and then consider the works of its best period till I become filled with the spirit of the ornament. For the time I have now become a Greek, or an Indian, or an Italian, as the case may be; and being in the right spirit, and having right feelings, I design, perhaps, new shapes, and new combinations of shapes, but to all they are obviously Greek, or Indian, or Italian, as the case may be. If they lack the desired spirit, then they cannot be employed.

I go farther, and say that it is not inconsistent to produce what we think the Greek, or the Egyptian, or any other people would have produced, had they possessed the knowledge of styles which we enjoy, provided that we give to all we do that character which the Greek or the Egyptian would have given.

In taking this latitude, the utmost care must be exercised in order that a merely mongrel style be not produced. The purest feeling of the style intended to be employed must be apparent in every new form, or the work is sure to be unsatisfactory; but in the hands of that man who can so imbue himself with the feelings of such men as must have designed old ornaments as to become for a time as one of them these licences may be taken with comparative safety.

In adopting an Historic style for the ornamentation of a house, it is not necessary to copy the faults of the style, nor is it desirable so to do. All fictitious relief in ornament I object to, for it is untruthful, but of this I will speak in another chapter. Much Italian ornament is painted in fictitious relief; all such I despise. But in order to discard what is false it is not necessary that we ignore the entire style. Italian ornament can be treated flatly, and having this consistent treatment its value is at once enhanced and no loss of effect is thereby induced; on the contrary, by this treatment it gains both power and boldness. When we apply a style of historic ornament to our wants, we do well to sift it, as we do ancient literature, and in ignoring what is impure, false, or degrading, we do well.

CHAPTER IX.

ON TRUTHFULNESS OF EXPRESSION IN ORNAMENTATION.

I WISH that "graining" had never been invented, for then wood-work would have been simply varnished, so that it may be kept clean, or painted of a colour such as would harmonise with the decorations and furniture of a room. "Graining" and "marbling" are both falsities, which must be condemned. Few marbles look well when two or more kinds are together, for it is almost impossible to get them of harmonising colours, and yet we constantly see imitations of various marbles made and combined together, while the ultimate end achieved is most unsatisfactory, and often even offensive. To all falsities, whether they produce a pleasant or an unpleasant effect, I alike object. All that is untrue is unworthy of art.

How can we expect our art to be cherished and to be loved unless it sets aside what is false? And how can we hope that it will exert a purifying influence upon those who study it if it be not true? We are the employers of a noble art, which has qualities capable of refining the tastes, the feelings, and the very natures of those who contemplate it. It must, then, be free from what is false. Truth must ever be the first principle in our creed, and with that man who will not join me in the effort at revealing truth in his every work I have no sympathy.

Flatness is an almost invariable characteristic of walls, and it is a welcome feature both of a wall and of a ceiling also; our decorations of these surfaces must therefore be flat, for it is our duty, as well as our privilege, to express truth. In the centres of many ceilings we find a plaster ornament in relief, but there is no attempt made at deception here, for the ornament is what it pretends to be. As these ornaments, as well as the modelled enrichments of most cornices, are usually almost devoid of art feeling, and are generally coarse and vulgar, I remove these before I commence the decoration of a room. I have no objection to modelled ornamentation; it is not false, and may be highly artistic, but a "rose" of artistic character is rarely found in the centre of a ceiling.

To ornaments, of whatever description, if in fictitious relief, I object. It is no more legitimate to make pieces of earthenware look like basket-work, or to make an

iron coal-box look as if made of wood, than it is to grain or to marble a door;
but all are false, and all are beneath the notice of an artist.

The truthful expression of the real character of a cornice is difficult for the
inexperienced to achieve, yet truth must be told.   A cornice consists of advancing, flat,
and receding members ; now, to give to each its due place is not an easy matter.   One
member advances beyond another ; when coloured it should appear to be forward.
One member retires behind another ; when coloured it should appear to be retiring.
The utmost knowledge is necessary to the attainment of what is here required.   To
cause one member to advance and another to recede in appearance is not difficult,
but to give to each its exact position requires much knowledge.   Of the colouring
of cornices I shall speak in detail in another chapter, but the laws that I shall there
enunciate will be those calculated to secure simple truthfulness of expression.

CHAPTER X.

ON THE VARIOUS WAYS IN WHICH ROOMS MAY BE DECORATED.

IN the worst days of Roman art ceilings and walls were decorated with festoons of leafage, delineations of cupolas in the wildest perspective, and other monstrosities as offensive in appearance as they were unsuitable to the purpose for which they were intended. As if intentionally to outrage even our commonest perception of what is right, the old Romans frequently painted on the insides of domes, and on the curved surfaces of covings, festoons of flowers bent upwards instead of hanging in a pendant manner. All such decorations are alike false, inconsistent, and coarse, and by them it is impossible that repose be attained.

The great Italian masters revived the style of the Romans, but instead of employing medallions, vignettes, and small caryatides upon the ceilings, they in many instances covered the entire surface with one painting; or, after panelling the ceiling in a fictitious manner, painted in each compartment a separate picture. It must ever be remembered that in order to the attainment of the highest merit in any work the entire energies of the life of its producer must be devoted to one study. Is it reasonable to suppose that a man could become as great a physician were he to devote half his time to the study of law as he would were he to devote his whole life to the consideration of diseases and their cures? But where a man is obviously fitted for one particular pursuit—say the study of engineering—is it likely that he will make a great artist by devoting half his time to art and only half to engineering? And would he not also be inferior as an engineer to what he would have been had his studies been undivided? It does not follow that because a man is great in his understanding of one branch of knowledge that he necessarily has great understanding of any other branch; and it is more than probable that if he divide his energies he will attain to imperfect knowledge of any one art, or branch of learning. The minds of the great Italian painters sought expression in pictorial art, and some of their works are of inexpressible loveliness, but their decorations manifest nothing but ignorance of their art, and in no one instance attain the realisation of repose in the apartment decorated. Raphael's arabesques in the Vatican at Rome are as false and feeble as the worst of the Roman productions; and even the ceiling of the

Sistine Chapel is, when considered from a decorative point of view, untrue in expression, and therefore inadmissible as a decorative work, and the effect attained by the application of all pictorial art to walls or ceilings is always unsatisfactory and uncomfortable.*

It was common to paint clouds and sky on ceilings in England at one time. Happily this false method of decoration has now disappeared, but the habit of dividing ceilings into fictitious architectural panels is not yet entirely abandoned, while it is untrue and altogether unnecessary to the attainment of the most desirable effects. A ceiling may be divided into compartments by flat ornamental members, in the manner that the Persians break up their compositions into parts, but here there is no simulation of architectural setting out.

A ceiling looks well if it has upon it a flat tint with a plain border of colour. It may be enriched by having a large centre ornament painted upon it, or further enriched by the addition of an ornamental border or a border and corners. If the cornice is broad it will serve for a sufficient bordering (frame) to the ceiling.

Walls are best not panelled, unless they are panelled by the architecture. Nevertheless, if a room is long and looks low the breaking up of the walls into narrow vertical portions will give apparent height. In other words, a long room looks lower than it is; by the employment of vertical lines on the wall it may be caused to look as high as it actually is. A wall may have a dado formed on its sides. This will give a sense of snugness, and if the room is long the dado will attract attention to its length. A wall, like a ceiling, may simply be bordered all round, as in the case of Persian and Moorish decorations, but this treatment accords only with the richest decorations. On the effects of these various modes of treatment I shall speak in other chapters.

* See my remarks upon this subject in " The Principles of Decorative Design," page 82.

CHAPTER XI.

ON THE NECESSITY FOR COLOURING AND DECORATING CEILINGS, AND ON MODES OF TREATING THEM.

I HAVE already said that "repose" cannot be achieved in a room unless the ceiling is coloured. A white patch in the centre of decorations prevents the attainment of that unity of effect which is the aim of the artist. A ceiling looks well if of plain blue of almost any depth. Pure ultramarine may be used if the room is well furnished with light. Light in an apartment is highly desirable, but there should be only a small amount of light reflected to the eye by the ceiling and walls, if the highest degree of repose is to be achieved. The ceiling may be of paler blue than pure ultramarine. About half way between pure ultramarine and white it looks well. It also looks well when of pale blue, but in this case the blue is better of grey tint. To the blue and white add a certain amount of raw Turkey umber: this will give softness to the tint. If simple corners are stencilled on this blue in any shade of cream-colour (form the cream-colour of a small portion of middle chrome, of orange chrome, and of white), it will look well. But the plain ceiling, with a well-coloured cornice, never looks offensive.

A ceiling looks well if of cream-colour. In this case rather light grey-blue corners may be stencilled upon it (Plate XLI.). Stars in grey-blue may also be stencilled upon it; but these will look better if of varying sizes, and with varying numbers of points. For rooms of about ten to fifteen feet in height, six-pointed stars, two to three inches in diameter, may be used; others of two to two and a half inches in diameter, with five points; others rather smaller, with the same number of points; others about one and a half inches in diameter, with four points; and others smaller, with only three points. Such stars placed irregularly (without order), but in somewhat equal distribution over the ceiling, always look well. The same arrangement of stars may occur on the blue ceilings, when the stars may be in cream-colour if the blue is not deep, or in a lighter shade of blue if the blue is deep.

A rich effect is always attained by painting on a ceiling a well-designed and harmoniously-coloured centre ornament, only the entire ceiling must be tinted. A pure cream-colour is, perhaps, the best for a ceiling if a rich centre is to be painted on it; and next to this a sort of drab or fawn-colour, such as that forming the ground of Plate XIII., but the centre must not be so small as to look insignificant. I often make them so large that they reach the cornice, within about a foot, at the centre of each side. The central ornament should rarely be less than about one-half the diameter of the ceiling, if it is to look rich.

There is little fear of colours, however positive in character, looking vulgar or strong on a ceiling, if they are but perfectly harmonious, and are used in only small masses. All decorative work must consist of small parts if refinement of effect is to be attained.

I rarely use corners when I have a rich centre. I prefer a larger centre and a rich cornice to a smaller centre and corners; and a larger centre can be employed if there are no corner ornaments than if there are. Plate XIII. gives a rich central ornament for the ceiling of a middle-sized room.

Much as I like a well-designed and harmoniously-coloured central ornament for a ceiling, I think the most perfect results are attained by an "all-over" pattern. As illustrations of this class of decoration I give Plates I., XLIII., XLIV., and XLIX. By this "all-over" treatment the ceiling can be rendered so "bloomy" in effect, and the whole apartment made so rich, so snug, and so cosy, that this method of treatment stands unrivalled for desirable qualities. The central ornament is a change, and may be a pleasant change, but the all-over decoration is that which enables us to achieve the highest art effects.

Simple ceilings of this character in blue and cream-colour always look well, and they are particularly suited to ordinary rooms, both sitting and sleeping rooms. As examples of such ceiling patterns I have given Plates XXX., XXXIII., XLIV., and XLIX.; but the pattern given on Plate XXX. is only suitable to corridors, as it will run in lines. Lines running throughout the length of a corridor are not objectionable on a ceiling.

With the decoration of a ceiling great care must be taken, for it is the only decorated surface in the room which can be seen in its entirety. "Quantities" are here most important, for it is not broken up, and in part hidden, by furniture, as the wall is. A carpet should be a complete and well-considered work, having invariably a border, and the border should be of proper proportion to the central portion or "filling"; but it is in part covered by table and chairs; hence any little defects in it are not readily perceived. It is not so with the ceiling, for it can be perfectly seen; hence the utmost care must be exercised, in order that its proportions be just, its ornaments suitable, and its general effect refined.

CHAPTER XII.

ON THE DECORATION OF WALLS.

IF gorgeousness of effect is desired, it is often necessary to cover the entire walls of a room with ornament; but here the primary colours should be employed, together with gold, in extremely small masses. In the Alhambra the effect of gorgeousness is well attained. Such effects are rarely called for in this country; and if their production is attempted by any other than a very competent artist, the result is almost sure to be vulgar. A fine effect is obtained by covering a wall with gold, and placing on this gold a small black figure—a cross, a cross and star, or some small running pattern, but in such a case much more gold than black should be visible (Plate XIX.).

When the surface of a wall is rich the wall may be bordered all round, or made into one panel, but the bordering must go almost close into the corners and to the skirting and cornice of the room, and not leave a "style" around. Plate XV. gives a plain bordering and corners for a wall, but this could be worked on a gold ground. On this gold and black ground pictures in ebony and gold frames look exceedingly well.

Perhaps the best treatment of walls is that of arranging a dado upon them. Let a room be twelve feet high. The cornice will take six inches from the top of the wall, and the skirting twelve or fourteen inches from the bottom. Let us now draw a line three feet above the skirting, or a little over four feet from the floor. The wall we make cream-colour; but the dado, or portion below the line, we paint maroon or chocolate. On this lower portion we place a pattern, say that of either figure on Plate XXIII. if the room is Greek, or of XVI. if it is Gothic, and the effect of our wall is now satisfactory.

A very small figure may be placed on the upper portion of the wall, or in some cases even a strong diaper pattern or spray (Plates VI., VIII., XX., XXIV., XXXVII., XLV.), but it is often more desirable to keep the upper part of the wall plain than it is to decorate it.

The upper portion of a dado must always consist of a band—the dado-rail. Plates V., VII., XIV., XVII., XXII., XXIX., XXXV., XLVI., XLVIII., LVII., give ornaments suitable for this purpose. The lower portion of the dado may be plain, or it may have a simple pattern stencilled upon it (Plate XII.), or it may be enriched to any extent (Plate XI., right lower corner). On the top of the dado-rail it is sometimes desirable to have an ornament falling on the wall-colour, and not on the dado-colour. Plate X. furnishes a rich ornament of this kind, suitable to work with XVII. as a dado-rail; but the dado would here require to be very rich and col"., coloury throughout. Simple ornaments in one or two colours may often be advantageously employed in a similar manner.

If pictures are to hang upon a wall, it is highly desirable that no pattern be placed on that portion of the wall against which the pictures are to rest. If a room in which pictures are to hang is high I often use a dado, and place around the wall a frieze, at a distance of about two feet or more below the cornice, and star the wall with gold stars above this frieze, or treat it in various ways. This treatment is satisfactory if the dado is kept heavier and stronger than the upper portion of the wall. Of friezes suitable to this position I give many examples. A cream-coloured wall comes well with a dark-blue dado. In this case the blue should not consist of pure ultramarine, but of ultramarine with a little black and a little white added to give a certain amount of neutrality. A ceiling must look pure, a wall somewhat neutral. A citrine wall, like the ground of Plates XXII., XLV. (upper figure), or V. (lower figure), looks well with a dark-blue dado. A grey-blue wall of middle tint looks well with a rich and slightly orange-maroon dado, as the blue of Plate XLI. with the plain maroon band in Plate XLVIII. Gold ornaments may be employed on this maroon dado with good effect. On the citrine wall both oil-paintings and water-colour drawings look well if in black frames with an inner gold beading. On the grey-blue background they look well in gold frames.

Dados may advantageously vary in height. In some cases they may with advantage be nearly two-thirds of the entire height of a room : this gives quaintness of effect. Their height should be governed by the degree of light in the room, and by the furniture. Furniture always looks best on a dark background—indeed, almost everything does; hence the desirability of having a dado. Dados may vary from eighteen inches to seven feet in height, according to circumstances.

A wall should never be divided into equal parts : if it is ten feet high the dado and skirting cannot possibly be five feet together, for this arrangement would look hideous. The more subtle, and difficult to detect, proportions are the better. A dado, in relation to the wall, may be as four to eleven, as seven to twelve, and so on, but not as three to six.

CHAPTER XIII.

ON THE WOOD-WORK OF ROOMS.

IF the wood-work of a room is simply varnished, or if stained and varnished, then the decorations of the walls and ceiling must harmonise with it, for it is a tint which we cannot alter; if, however, it is painted, then it can be coloured as may be required.

Whatever acts as a frame to something else is better darker than that which it frames, or in some way stronger in effect. A cornice, as the frame of a ceiling, should be stronger in effect than the ceiling; in like manner, a skirting, which frames the floor, should always be dark. I have never yet seen a room which was altogether satisfying to the eye where the skirting was light. A white skirting should never exist. I often make the skirting black, but in this case I generally polish or varnish the greater portion of it, yet leave parts " dead," thus getting a contrast between a bright and a dead surface. I sometimes run a few lines of colour upon its mouldings, but I never in any way ornament it. It should be retiring and bold in effect, hence its treatment must be simple. If not black, it may often advantageously be brown, rich maroon, dull blue, or bronze-green. Even in light rooms it should be considerably darker than the walls. A dark colour gives the idea of strength; that portion of a wall on which weight appears specially to rest, should be dark.

I like to see the wood-work of a room generally of darker tint than the walls. A door should always be conspicuous; it should never be hidden as if its existence was not desirable. I find that a room almost invariably looks better when the doors are darker, rather than lighter, than the walls; and the advantage of dark architraves must be obvious to all who have tried them. A door should rarely, perhaps never, be of the colour of the wall, even if of darker tint; this is a resort of those who cannot form a harmony with the wall-colour. If a wall is citrine, the door may be dark low-toned Antwerp-blue, or it may be of dark bronze-green ; but in this latter case, a line of red should be run round the inside of the architrave : if the wall is blue, a dark orange-green will do well for the door, but a line of red around this door will improve it, or the door may be an orange-maroon. If the wall is bright turquoise in colour, the door may be Indian-red (vermilion brought to a beautiful tertiary shade with ultramarine). These are mere illustrations of numerous harmonious combinations which may be made, but they serve to show my meaning.

The architraves of doors may often be of hand-polished black with advantage, or consist in part of bright and in part of " dead " black. The bright work should always be of the best character, yet good varnished work looks well. If the architraves of doors are black, one or two lines of colour may be run upon them ; if the lines are very narrow, say the one-sixteenth of an inch in width, they may be of the brightest colours ; if broad, say three-quarters of an inch, they should be much subdued in tone, and hardly brighter in tint than the colour of the wall.

If the windows of a room are recessed so that six inches or more of the thickness of the wall occur on the inside of the room, by painting this recess dark, and by making the architrave of bright black, such an effect of snugness is induced that if amber blinds are employed for the window instead of white, no curtains will appear to be necessary. Thus if the walls are of cream-colour, with maroon dado, paint the shutters or the thickness of the wall bronze-green, or the tertiary " olive," and make the shutter box, or architrave, bright black, with perhaps a line of colour—say a line of red. The effect will have a completeness which is in itself satisfying.

I rarely find it necessary to decorate the panels of doors or shutters, and I never place ornaments on the "styles." If an ornament is placed on a panel, it is better quaint and slightly heraldic in appearance, as the circular ornaments on Plate IV. A monogram may in some cases be applied to a door, but it must not be frequently repeated.

The sashes of a window should almost invariably be of bright black internally ; they will not then attract to themselves attention, which they will do if of light colour. We want to see through a window, and not have our attraction arrested by the sashes.

CHAPTER XIV.

ON CORNICES.

NOTHING in the way of decoration is so difficult as rightly to colour a cornice. Each member occupies a particular place, and has a particular sectional form: we have so to colour the cornice that every member shall appear to be in its proper position, and look to be exactly what it really is. Colour enables us to give to objects a charm which they would not have without it; it also assists in the manifestation of form, but by its agency we can often express truth or falsity. We must ever strive after the expression of truth.

No one having art-knowledge would ever apply to a cornice the colours of the wall-decorations simply because they are wall-colours. A cornice is the frame to the ceiling, and the uppermost boundary of a wall; it should therefore be stronger in effect than the wall. It also is much smaller as a quantity than either walls or ceiling, it may therefore be more coloury in effect.

Strong colours may generally be used with advantage on a cornice—even pure vermilion, carmine, and ultramarine. But with these colours it is often necessary to have a much paler, and somewhat grey, shade of blue; and it is generally necessary to have also a soft shade of yellow (formed of middle-chrome and white), not a raw-looking yellow, together with white, gold, or black.

Yellow is an advancing colour; gold, by its glitter, is also advancing; these colours should therefore be used on advancing, or convex, members (gold, if used on a cornice, should never be burnished: indeed, burnished gold should never occur in house decoration). If gold is applied to the flat members of a cornice, its effect is almost lost. Red, as a colour, is about stationary; that is, a red object looks neither nearer nor farther from us than it actually is; it should, therefore, be used chiefly on flat surfaces. It looks best in shade, in light it is too attractive; hence such surfaces as are in shadow are best adapted for the reception of this colour. Blue is a receding colour; it is adapted for hollows, as covings and concave mouldings.

Now the difficulty in colouring a cornice rests in our having to render every member distinct, and in so modifying our yellows, blues, and reds, or whatever colours we employ, as to cause each separate member to appear to advance or recede to the exact extent that it actually does. We have said that colour has to assist form. If a cornice is uncoloured, it is often impossible to judge of its sectional shape. If properly coloured, the nature of its mouldings should be apparent.

If there are flat members in a cornice of an inch and a half or more in breadth, these may be enriched with simple patterns in blue and white, or red and white, or in any colours demanded by the situation of the member; a coving, if sufficiently large, may also be enriched. Mere vertical lines of colour look well in this position, and are useful in showing the precise curve of the coving.

Care must always be taken not to cause a cornice to look liney; there must be a certain amount of "breadth" of treatment. If the cornice only consists of narrow lines, it cannot look well. There must be comparatively broad members, as well as those which are narrow.

It is often necessary that the colours employed in the decoration of a cornice, especially if they be "primaries," be separated from each other by a white line, or by a white member. Red and blue, if of the same depth, produce a "swimmy" effect if juxtaposed, and the production of this dazzling is rarely desirable; it is prevented, however, by a white line interposing between them.

The principles that apply to the colouring of cornices also apply to the treatment of all relief ornament. Red is best in shadow, blue on receding surfaces, yellow on advancing members.

CHAPTER XV.

ON THE NECESSITY FOR HARMONY BETWEEN ALL THE PARTS OF A ROOM.

No one will doubt the necessity for the existence of harmony between all the decorations of a room. It is not sufficient that the ceiling be decorated with the same style of ornament as the walls, nor that the whole of the ornament be designed in the same spirit, for a colour harmony must result from the contrast of all the colours of the room, and the result achieved must be *repose*.

Harmony between the various decorations can be achieved in many ways. A ceiling in which blue prevails, or even a plain blue ceiling, a suitably coloured cornice, citrine walls, and a rich maroon dado will produce a harmony. A ceiling of blue-green general effect, walls of low-toned yellow orange, and a dado of deep red-purple will produce a harmony. In both these cases the doors might be of bronze-green, and the architraves black. Purple, although in some cases useful, can but seldom be used with advantage in house decoration. As a colour it is too attractive or obtrusive to be lavishly used.

Direct harmonies between the various decorations of a room are not so desirable as those which are more subtle or intricate in character; and as the complexity of the decorative scheme increases, a necessarily greater amount of skill is requisite to their being satisfactorily carried out.

A plain blue ceiling, I have said, will harmonise with a citrine wall and a maroon dado; but if the ceiling decoration presents various pure colours so arranged that its general hue is olive, and the wall ornaments are formed of bright colours so disposed that they yield a citrine tint, and the dado is made up of such an admixture of colours that the general tone is russet, the three will together produce a harmony, for olive, citrine, and russet are the three tertiary colours, and they together form a harmony; and the harmony thus produced will be refined, intricate, and peculiarly pleasant to dwell upon.

When rooms open one into the other, it is often desirable to give to one a general citrine hue, to another a russet hue, and to another an olive hue; for in such a case the three, when seen through the openings which lead from one to the other, produce a harmony.

If there are but two rooms adjoining, one may have a red hue, and the other a green hue; or one may have a blue tone, and the other an orange tone; in either of which case a harmony will be produced.

It must be specially noticed that we speak of hues and tones of colour only, and not of positive tints, which are always too strong for walls. Walls are the backgrounds on which our furniture is seen, on which our paintings are hung, and from which the occupants of a room are to derive enhanced effects of comeliness and beauty; they cannot then be positive in colour. Blue, being a retiring colour, may be used in greater intensity than red; and red, being a stationary colour, in a stronger hue than yellow, for yellow is always advancing; but all backgrounds must be more or less neutral, yet the neutrality may result from the use of tertiary colours or from the use of extremely small parts of pure pigments in their intensity.

A room can rarely look well if its walls are of bright green. Green is a colour that must be sparingly used in decoration: it should be employed only by the skilful decorator, for it is apt to look coarse and vulgar. If a room looks upon grass, trees, or a garden, its walls should never be green, for the artist must seek to so arrange his work that Nature will always look lovely; if, however, the walls of a room which commands a beautiful landscape are green, neither the landscape nor the walls can look well.

CHAPTER XVI.

ON THE SUITABLE DECORATION OF ROOMS INTENDED FOR VARIOUS PURPOSES.

SOME persons feel the necessity of making rooms different from one another, because of the various uses to which they are applied, more strongly than I do. Variety is said to be charming. This I fully admit; but I cannot see that one room should be necessarily dark, and another necessarily almost white, when the two rooms are used to sit in.

My experience leads me to the conclusion that the finest art effects are attainable where the colouring is of middle depth. A very dark room is rarely desirable, and about a very light room there is a want of that snugness and repose in the absence of which the higher art effects cannot exist. Yet it is not necessary that all rooms be of equal depth. We must avoid that lightness which entails an absence of colour. There is no art manifested where the decorations are white and gold, for no repose is achieved. Colour lends to objects a charm which they could not have without it. To deprive ourselves of a source of pleasure, by making our rooms white, or grey and white, instead of combinations of harmonious colours, is like insisting only on melody in music and excluding harmony.

I am not astonished at the fact that many persons have grey and white drawing-rooms when I think of the hideous effects which I sometimes have shown me as decorations, where perhaps a pale emerald green, a grey, and a ghastly pink—the very pink that will not harmonise with the crude green in question—are the colours employed. The hideousness of some decorations, so called, is beyond expression, and white walls are infinitely preferable to such. Many persons are colour-blind. The late Professor George Wilson, of Edinburgh, ascertained by experiment that one person out of every ten sees colour imperfectly, and that one in every forty cannot see colour at all. In charity I will suppose that some of our, so-called, decorators are colour-blind, and I think that there is every reason to suppose that such is the case. Such persons cannot, by any process of cultivation, become colourists. They may draw perfectly, and have the keenest perception of light and shade, but they must leave the colouring of their designs to others.

A dining-room we generally make rather dark. The table, when set for a repast, certainly looks better if the surroundings are of a receding character. Citrine, or blue of medium depth, and with greyish hue, looks well for the wall of a dining-room, and a maroon dado is very suitable. It is desirable that the spread table and the viands have prominence given to them by the shade of the walls. But our table-cloths are too strong in effect. Instead of being white, they should be of cream-tint, for the general repose would not then be disturbed by them, and yet the table would have sufficient prominence given to it. The emblems of the feast—fish, birds, and beasts—may sometimes be incorporated with the decoration of a dining-room with advantage, but these must be drawn in a conventional manner.

The effect of lightness is usually given to drawing-rooms. I think that we generally make these rooms too light; we give to them a coldness which is freezing, rather than that depth of tint which gives snugness, and that cheerfulness which promotes conversation. Furniture cannot look well against a very light wall, and excessive lightness of tint produces a mere sense of whiteness, and against this as a background every object seems cut out with offensive sharpness and hardness.

Bed-rooms are wrongly made very light. The decorations of a bed-room should be eminently soothing. In the hour of sickness we all feel this. It is not whiteness or dazzle that we want; it is that which is soothing and which conduces to rest. There must be an absence of spots, or specially attractive features, from all good decoration, but in a bed-room this is especially necessary.

A smoking-room, or "sanctum," is the one room where we may indulge in the grotesque and humorous. Here it is not inconsistent to perpetuate such extravagances as will provoke mirth, but the grotesque must always be clever and vigorous. Feeble grotesques must be avoided.

In these days of competition, when the brain is ever active, and the nerve force is kept for many hours together in constant play, it is peculiarly desirable that our rooms be soothing in effect and snugy in appearance: and that degree of richness which is necessary to the destruction of coldness and poverty of appearance is much to be desired in all our rooms. If special richness is to be indulged in, bestow it upon the library.

CHAPTER XVII.

ON THE TREATMENT OF THE GROTESQUE.

IN ornament humour finds expression in the grotesque. Humour is no new characteristic of the human race; it is as old and as natural as love. This being the case, we find the grotesque in all styles of ornament, but in some it predominates, while in others it is of rare occurrence. A curious manifestation of the grotesque is to be found in Celtic ornament, where the majority of the forms employed are monstrosities of some description. Professor Westwood, in his beautiful work on Celtic ornament, gives some fine illustrations of old Celtic manuscripts in which this class of ornament prevails: these are well worthy of careful study. It will be noticed that while Celtic ornament consists almost wholly of grotesques, no attempt is made at the representation of natural objects. We discern birds and beasts and fishes, but the bird is not a sparrow, nor a snipe, nor a partridge, nor, indeed, any specific kind of bird. Such characters are given as convey to the mind the thought of a bird, but all specific characteristics are studiously avoided. In some cases the neck of a bird, or the body of a beast, is formed of strap-work; and two animals are not unfrequently twined together in a curious and intricate manner. All this is perfectly right, for the whole composition is ornamental and not naturalistic, and the effect produced is highly humorous. In the present work Plate VI. gives illustrations of this class of grotesque.

Grotesques should never be very naturalistic in treatment; and if in any distorted or unnatural position, they should be obviously unreal in character. The production in decorative art of anything that appears always to be suffering pain should be carefully avoided.

In the present work I give grotesques of various characters, some of which come as near to nature as is consistent with the canons of decoration.

In my " Principles of Decorative Design " I have considered grotesques, and I must refer the student to that little work for further information on this subject; but, to summarise the laws which govern the production of " monsters " in ornament, we may say,—

1. The farther the grotesque is removed from a natural representation of what is

intended the better it is, provided that those characters are adopted which render the purpose of the representation at once obvious.

2. The drawing of all grotesques must be vigorous and energetic. Grotesques must be expressed with such force and power as will give to them apparent reality, however impossible their formation may be. Grotesques are to ornament what humour is to literature. Nothing is worse than a feeble joke; in like manner a feeble grotesque can only be despicable. The amusing must appear to be earnest.

3. A grotesque must reveal, by its nature or formation, knowledge on the part of its producer. Humour, to be acceptable to the educated, must be accompanied with the manifestation of knowledge. An ignorant joke is unpleasant to the educated even if the wit be obvious; in like manner all grotesques must reveal the knowledge of their producers, and be of such a character as shall show that their producers were men of learning.

CHAPTER XVIII.

ON COMBINATIONS OF THE EXAMPLES GIVEN IN THE PRESENT WORK.

IN the present work I have sought to accomplish two ends. First, I have endeavoured to give actual examples of decorative work; and second, I have attempted to furnish what I may term food for thought, and suggestions for original compositions.

To all who are qualified to be decorators the latter will be the more useful purpose of the work; and should my examples be considered *outré* or eccentric, which some undoubtedly will be, I yet hope that, if reasoned upon, they will be seen to express knowledge of the principles of historic art, grace, vigour, or some quality which may render them worthy of consideration.

In furnishing suggestions to others, I think it advisable often to accentuate certain qualities so that they may be very apparent—even too conspicuous to be pleasant, for they then become "striking" features; and when once attention has been drawn to a principle, it can readily be perceived even if but just hinted at.

I will now proceed to give certain combinations of examples found in my present book which might be useful for various purposes. A dado like Plate XVI. might have a wall of the same colour, and on this wall might be stencilled either of the "powderings" given on Plates VI. or XXIV. in suitable colours. If a frieze is required, it might be either of those on Plate LVII. or the lower bordering on Plate XIV.; but whichever frieze is used must be altered in colour, and made in this respect similar to those on Plate XXIX. With these walls either of the ceilings on Plates XXI. or L. will look well; so also will the plainer ceiling given on Plate XLIV. As another room, let the dado be as the darker pattern on Plate XXXIX.; the dado-rail as the chameleon border on Plate XIV.; the walls as any pattern on Plate XXVII. (in this case the cream-coloured members of the dado pattern might be the same yellow as the wall), or as the lighter pattern on Plate XXXIX.; and the ceiling as Plate XLIX. As another room, let the dado be plain chocolate; the dado-rail be as the lower bordering on Plate XXII. (the chocolate of the dado would have to be of precisely the same shade of colour as that employed in the dado-rail).

The wall to be a tertiary yellow, similar in colour to the ground of the dado-rail ; *
and plain if pictures are to be hung on it, or figured with such a "powdering" as one
of those on Plate XXXVII. if there are to be no pictures and a certain elaboration
of effect is required.   Plate XL. may be studied for colours which harmonise with
a tertiary yellow ground.   The frieze may be as the upper bordering on Plate
XXII., and any of the four ceiling patterns given on Plates XXI. or L. will look well
with these walls ; so also will a plain blue ceiling ; or if the room is small, a plain
blue ceiling, with the figure given on Plate LV. as a centre ornament.   If a more
simple effect is required, the ceilings given on Plates XXXIII. or XLIX. might
be employed.

Plate XXXIV. gives the frieze for Plate XIX.   The upper border on Plate
XXXV. would look well in any two simple colours, provided that they are harmonious ;
or in black on red. as Plate XIV. ; on tertiary yellow, as the ground of Plate XL. ; on
chocolate, as the ground of Plate XXIII. ; or on yellow, as Plate XXVII. ; and the same
will apply to all the other patterns in two colours only.   Every example which is
given in this book must be regarded as a study in colour combination, and it is only
by individual research that satisfactory use can be made of ornamental illustrations.

* Pictures or engravings in black frames look well on this back ground.

CHAPTER XIX.

ON METHODS OF DECORATING ROOMS.

WALL-PAPERS are the means whereby the decoration of the great majority of rooms is accomplished. The objection to the use of wall-papers rests chiefly in their joining by vertical lines. If the sides of the strips were cut to the pattern so that the projections of one side fitted to the indentations in the other, the chief objection to the employment of paper-hangings would be removed. This is done with heavy flock papers, and it should be done in all rooms where anything more than mere cleanliness is required.

One hindrance to this mode of hanging papers arises in the fact that but few paper-hangers can cut a paper with a reasonable degree of accuracy if they have to follow the pattern. I have been many times discouraged with the want of ability of this kind on the part of workmen, and have cut the papers myself rather than have them spoiled. Scissors cannot cut the true and delicate curves that it is often necessary to follow. A sharp knive can alone be employed for this purpose; and the paper should rest on hard glass, so that the knife may be perfectly under the control of the cutter, and not diverted by "grain" as when the paper is cut on wood.

I see no objection whatever to the use of wall-papers for the decoration of ordinary rooms, provided they are used as decorations, and not merely as so much material with which the walls are to be covered. One paper may form a dado, and another the wall covering. But in this case there must always be a dado-rail—which should be somewhat bold and effective—intervening between the wall and dado, and of the colours of the dado, or of colours forming a harmony with it. Around the top of the room there must be a frieze, if there is little or no cornice, and the ceiling must have a pattern upon it. All this can be properly done by the use of paper decorations, only the choice of suitable ornaments must be as carefully made as if the decorations were being designed especially for the room.* A paper dado with the wall of plain tint always looks well. Above the dado-rail a slight ornament may be stencilled on the wall-colour with the view of softening the

* Messrs. Jeffrey and Co., of Essex Road, Islington, have published a series of my decorations expressly to meet the requirements set forth in this work, each having my name printed on the margin of the strip.

abruptness with which the dado would otherwise fall on the wall, but this is by no means necessary. If the wall is to be of plain tint, I prefer the employment of "tempera" ("distemper") colour to either oil or "flatting." The surface of tempera work is so dead and solid that it is more pleasant to look upon than that even of the best flatting. If a wall is of tempera, and there is a high dado, there is but little fear of its being much rubbed or soiled. I advise that ordinary rooms have a dado of wall-paper (which should be hung horizontally and not in vertical strips), that the dado-rail be of paper, that the wall be a plain tempera tint, that the frieze be paper, that any flat members or large covings in the cornice be enriched with paper ornaments, and that the ceiling be covered with paper. The ceiling-paper must be of special character: a mere wall pattern placed on a ceiling looks horrible. Ceilings in grey and white, and similar pale tints, cannot look well. The ceiling pattern must have a certain amount of "strength" in its effect. (See Plates I., XIII., XXI., and XXXIII.)

A room could be decorated in this manner at about the same cost as if the wall were covered all over with a good "gold paper;" and in the one case a rich and decorated effect would be produced, and in the other a mere ordinary and inartistic room. If decoration is to become general in the country, it must be made popular by the intelligence and skill of our decorators.

The lower part of the wall must in some cases be washable. Thus in a bath-room both a wall-paper and a tempera wall are alike unsuitable. A common wall-paper if varnished rarely looks well, so I have little liking for this mode of treatment. A tempera wall, with a high plain dado in flatting colour, is what I generally employ for a bed-room. If the tempera is of cream tint, and the dado is of red maroon, and is separated from the cream-colour by a broad line or a double line of black, the effect is sure to be pleasant. The dado of a bath-room may be of oil colour, but it should not be varnished, and the wall may be " flatted."

If lasting decorations are required, and the conditions under which they are to exist are favourable to long existence, no one would think of using paper as a means of enrichment. Hand work is more durable if tempera colours are employed than if oil paints are used. The ceiling of a house standing far from any large town or smoky manufactory will, if decorated with tempera colours, look fresh for many years —even after decorations in oil would have become indistinct ; and even in a town the tempera decoration remains fresh longer than those in oil if it is so situated that it cannot be rubbed. The decorations of the old Egyptians which are still preserved to us are in tempera colours.

CHAPTER XX.

SUMMARY AND CONCLUSION.

THE progress of the decorative art rests largely with ourselves. I now speak to decorators. If we make our works worthy of patronage, I believe that patronage will be bestowed upon them. I am often perfectly amazed at the conduct of decorators when they are requested to commence the ornamentation of a room, and can only explain their mode of action by assuming their utter ignorance of the art which they profess to practise. They, upon seeing their client, ask how the room is to be treated. "Do you," they say, "wish a wall-paper?" "Shall it be a gold wall-paper?" "Do you wish the room light or dark?" "I will send you up a number of papers to choose from, and you can select which you please!" Such utterances can only spring from gross ignorance or a foolish timidity. What should we think if, when a medical man is called to see us, he asked how we would like the complaint treated; what medicine we desire; and if a tonic, whether we would have bark or arsenic? The decoration of a room is as much bound by laws and by knowledge as the treatment of a disease. A surgeon would not cut off an arm simply because a patient asked him so to do; he would first ascertain whether it was curable. I have no knowledge of the treatment of diseases; hence I commit myself to the care of a physician. I have no understanding of law; hence I employ a solicitor. I am called in to decorate a room; the client is as ignorant of my art as I am of his. Is it not my duty, then, to tell him that the room would look well if treated in such a way; or that its walls might be of such a colour? If we have understanding of our art, it is easy to convince others, who are ignorant, that we have more knowledge of the subject than they have; but we must be able to show a reason for the suggestions that we make.

Let it ever be borne in mind that every successful work executed by a man is an advertisement of his knowledge and skill, and that such tends to ennoble or exalt him; and that every work that he does which is offensive, untrue, or degrading—no matter who has dictated it—tends to his debasement, and is an advertisement of what can only be censured and should be avoided.

I look to decorators becoming the great teachers of art in the country. If we, as ornamentists, get knowledge, and explain to our clients why we propose treating their rooms in a particular manner, they will readily consent to the production of artistic rooms; and when once they have lived in an artistic house, they will never again like the white ceiling and merely papered walls, for their tastes will have improved.

Let us do all we can to exert an influence such as shall conduce to the rapid advancement of art amongst us. Let us make our decorations as durable as possible, for that which often wants renewing will never grow in favour. A decorated ceiling will last clean much longer than one that is white: it is, then, an economy to have such. Honest work, which is the expression of knowledge, when associated with the gentlemanly bearing of the decorator, and gentle persuasion, will accomplish all that we seek to achieve.

THE END.

Cassell Petter & Galpin, Belle Sauvage Works, London, E.C.
1275

STUDIES IN
DESIGN

PLATE I.

Ornament in the Arabian style, intended to be painted in the centre of a ceiling.

Dᴿ DRESSER Inv.

A. GOATER, LITHO. NOTTM.

STUDIES IN DESIGN—PLATE I.

Published by CASSELL, PETTER & GALPIN.

PLATE II.

" Parental advice" may be painted on the panel of a door, on the door of a cabinet, or in any recess in a wall, especially suited to a smoking-room or nursery.

A. GOATER, LITHO. NOTTM.

STUDIES IN DESIGN—PLATE II.

DR. DRESSER, INV.

Published by CASSELL, PETTER & GALPIN.

PLATE III.

A frieze of new style. This would be used around the upper part of the wall of a room. Being small in detail, it must not be placed high, unless it is enlarged.

DR. DRESSER, INV.

A. GOATER, LITHO. NOTTM.

Published by CASSELL, PETTER & GALPIN.

STUDIES IN DESIGN — PLATE III.

PLATE IV.

Two circular compositions of new style : may be used on the doors of cabinets, or as fillings for circular openings in a frieze.

A. GOATER, LITHO. NOTTM

Published by CASSELL, PETTER & GALPIN.

STUDIES IN DESIGN — PLATE IV.

PLATE V.

Border ornaments of new style. The upper may run around the architrave of a door or window, or be used in many ways as a border. The lower is suitable for a dado-rail, or, if enlarged, for a frieze.

A. GOATER, LITHO. NOTTM.

Published by CASSELL, PETTER & GALPIN.

STUDIES IN DESIGN — PLATE V.

PLATE VI.

Grotesque " powderings," suitable for the wall ornaments of a smoking-room. Owls, being regarded as typical of wisdom, are appropriate to a library or study.

Dr. Dresser, Inv.

A. GOATER, LITHO. NOTTM.

STUDIES IN DESIGN—PLATE VI.

Published by CASSELL, PETTER & GALPIN.

PLATE VII.

Grotesque dado-rail. Being formed of the hare, this is specially suited to a dining-room. Various animals may be introduced in a similar manner.

Published by CASSELL, PETTER & GALPIN

STUDIES IN DESIGN—PLATE VII.

PLATE VIII.

Diaper patterns founded on flowers. These are suitable for stencilling on the walls of rooms. They may be varied, and even simplified, in colour.

Dr. Dresser, Inv.

A. Goater, Litho. Nottm.

Published by CASSELL, PETTER & GALPIN.

Studies in Design—Plate VIII.

Dr. DRESSER, Inv.

A GOATER, LITHO. NOTTM.

STUDIES IN DESIGN — PLATE IX.

Published by CASSELL, PETTER & GALPIN.

PLATE X.

Ornament somewhat Indian in style ; to stand on top of dado-rail, falling upon a dark maroon wall.

STUDIES IN DESIGN—PLATE X.

Published by CASSELL, PETTER & GALPIN.

PLATE XI.

Outline studies. Two are for dividing a wall into panels. It is rarely advisable to break up a wall in this manner, unless this has been done by the architecture. The larger is semi-Moresque in character; the smaller is Gothic. In the right corner is a sketch for a dado in Gothic style.

STUDIES IN DESIGN—PLATE XI.

Published by CASSELL, PETTER & GALPIN.

PLATE XII.

Two patterns for dadoes, or the walls of small lobbies.

DR. DRESSER, INV.

A. GOATER, LITHO. NOTT'M.

Published by CASSELL, PETTER & GALPIN. STUDIES IN DESIGN—PLATE XII.

Published by CASSELL, PETTER & GALPIN.

STUDIES IN DESIGN—PLATE XIII.

PLATE XIV.
Two grotesque dado-rails.

Dr. DRESSER, Inv.

A. GOATER, LITHO. NOTTM.

Published by CASSELL, PETTER & GALPIN.

STUDIES IN DESIGN—PLATE XIV.

PLATE XV.

Bordering and corner. This may be used around the wall of a room; or, better, around that part of a wall which is above a dado.

Published by CASSELL, PETTER & GALPIN.

STUDIES IN DESIGN—PLATE XV.

PLATE XVI.

Design for a dado and dado-rail, of Gothic spirit, but not with the marked features of any style. Strongly horizontal in treatment, and calculated to give length, but not height, to a room.

STUDIES IN DESIGN—PLATE XVI.

Published by CASSELL, PETTER & GALPIN.

PLATE XVII.

Design for frieze, but may be used as rail of rich dado. If used as a frieze, the lines should be double below as they are above.

Dr. DRESSER, INV.

A. GOATER, LITHO. NOTTM.

Published by CASSELL, PETTER & GALPIN.

STUDIES IN DESIGN—PLATE XVII.

PLATE XVIII.

Design for wall or dado pattern. The flowers are all geometrically arranged on a square basis, and would appear as a regular powdering. The scroll-work is not geometrical in character. This class of pattern is difficult to do, but generally looks interesting.

DR. DRESSER, INV.

A. GOATER. LITHO. NOTTM.

Published by CASSELL, PETTER & GALPIN.

STUDIES IN DESIGN—PLATE XVIII.

PLATE XIX.

Wall pattern. The idea of this design was derived from the frost on a window-pane in winter. The style is new. Pictures in gold and black frames look well on this class of back-ground.

DR. DRESSER, INV.

A. GOATER, LITHO. NOTTM.

Published by CASSELL, PETTER & GALPIN.

STUDIES IN DESIGN—PLATE XIX.

PLATE XX.

Powderings. Suited for stencilling on walls and dadoes. They may be in any simple colours, and look especially well in black on orange-chocolate.

DR. DRESSER, INV.

A. GOATER LITHO. NOTTM.

STUDIES IN DESIGN—PLATE XX.

Published by CASSELL, PETTER & GALPIN.

PLATE XXI.

A rich ceiling-pattern, shown in two ways. The pattern should repeat, so that the maroon points (in the upper figure) would meet.

DR DRESSER, INV.

A. GOATER, LITHO. NOTTM.

STUDIES IN DESIGN—PLATE XXI.

Published by CASSELL, PETTER & GALPIN.

PLATE XXII.

Two frieze ornaments, or dado-rails. The style is peculiarly that of the Author. The citrine, which is the ground of these two borders, is an excellent colour for the walls of a library or dining-room. A maroon, or dark-blue, dado may be used with it; and pictures in black and gold frames come well upon it.

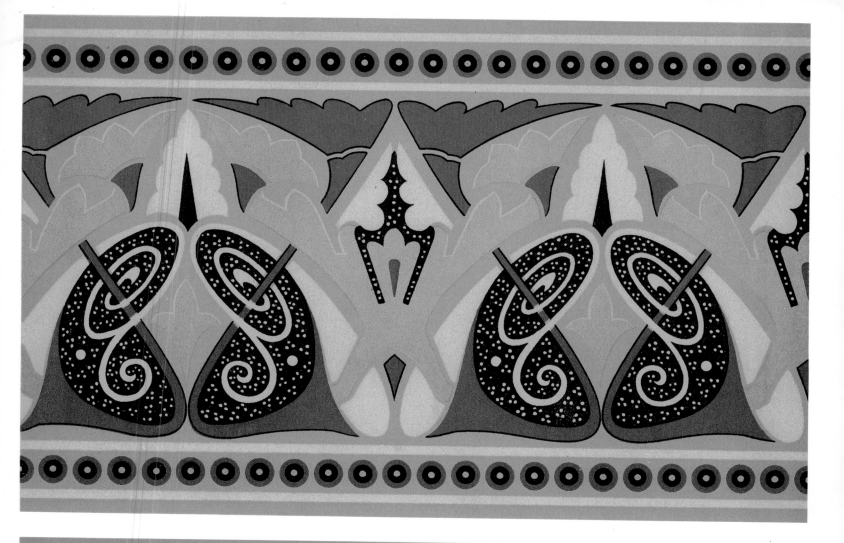

Published by CASSELL, PETTER & GALPIN.

STUDIES IN DESIGN—PLATE XXII.

PLATE XXIII.

Greek ornaments, suitable for dadoes ; but they require enlarging considerably.

Dr. Dresser, Inv

Published by CASSELL, PETTER & GALPIN.

Studies in Design—Plate XXIII.

A. GOATER, LITHO. NOTT'M.

PLATE XXIV.

Powderings. Suited for walls or dadoes. The corn is specially adapted for a dining-room.

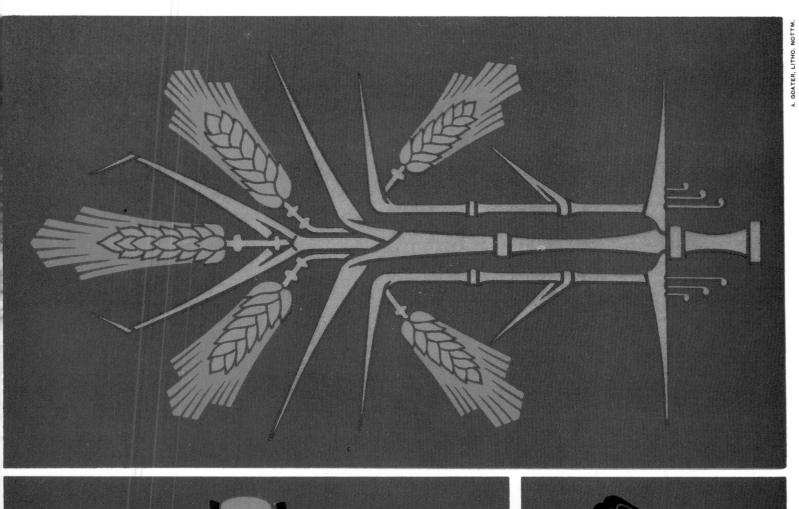

DR. DRESSER, INV.

A. GOATER, LITHO. NOTTM.

STUDIES IN DESIGN—PLATE XXIV.

Published by CASSELL, PETTER & GALPIN.

PLATE XXV.

Ornament for centre of small panel. It may be regarded as especially a study of colours harmonious with the ground on which they fall.

A. GOATER. LITHO. NOTTM.

Published by CASSELL, PETTER & GALPIN

STUDIES IN DESIGN—PLATE XXV.

PLATE XXVII.

Diaper patterns, especially suited for dadoes. They must be enlarged, unless the rooms to which they are applied are very small.

DR DRESSER INV

A. GOATER. LITHO. NOTTM.

PLATE XXVIII.

Design for central ornament of a ceiling. Style, Arabian. This would be painted upon the flat surface, and not cast in relief.

STUDIES IN DESIGN—PLATE XXVIII.

Published by CASSELL, PETTER & GALPIN.

PLATE XXIX.

Two dado-rail ornaments. Style, pure Arabian. Either would do well as a frieze also, but if the room was high both would require enlarging. The lower should be considerably larger if the room is more than twelve feet high; and about half as large again if the room is ten feet in height.

Studies in Design—Plate XXIX.

PLATE XXX.

A ceiling pattern. This hangs in lines, and is therefore adapted only for passages and long narrow rooms. In maroon, or low-toned yellow, and black, it would make a dado for the large hall of a business house.

A. Goater, Litho. Nottm.

Studies in Design—Plate XXX.

Published by Cassell, Petter & Galpin.

PLATE XXXI.

Two frieze or dado-rail ornaments, suitable for a drawing-room. Borderings of this class may sometimes be used advantageously around ceilings, either when the room is without cornice or when the cornice is very narrow

DR. DRESSER, INV.

A. GOATER, LITHO. NOTTM.

Published by CASSELL, PETTER & GALPIN.

STUDIES IN DESIGN—PLATE XXXI.

PLATE XXXII.

Three outline frieze ornaments, in free Gothic style. The lower may be used especially for ecclesiastical purposes, the head of any saint being employed. The right-hand outline is for the wall of a vestibule where quaintness is desired. Style, Gothic.

MINERVAM·EXCOLENDAM·
ARIOSTO

STUDIES IN DESIGN—PLATE XXXII.

PLATE XXXIII.

Ceiling-pattern in blue and white, suitable for a small, dark sitting-room.

Dr. DRESSER, Inv

Published by CASSELL, PETTER & GALPIN STUDIES IN DESIGN—PLATE XXXIII.

PLATE XXXIV.

Frieze suited to a room about fourteen feet high. Style new, the ornament being derived from the frost on a window-pane in winter. It would "work" well with Plate XIX. as a wall.

DR. DRESSER, INV.

A. GOATER LITHO. NOTT^{M.}

STUDIES IN DESIGN—PLATE XXXIV.

Published by CASSELL, PETTER & GALPIN.

PLATE XXXV.

Dado rails. This colouring could only be used where there are no plants or trees within view, as in a city, but even here should be but sparingly employed.

Published by CASSELL, PETTER & GALPIN.

STUDIES IN DESIGN—PLATE XXXV.

PLATE XXXVI

Pattern for wall.

Dr. DRESSER, Inv.

A. GOATER LITHO. NOTTM.

STUDIES IN DESIGN—PLATE XXXVI.

Published by CASSELL, PETTER & GALPIN.

PLATE XXXVII.

Sheet of powderings, adapted for wall-ornaments.

DR. DRESSER, INV.

A. GOATER, LITHO. NOTTM.

Published by CASSELL, PETTER & GALPIN.

STUDIES IN DESIGN—PLATE XXXVII.

PLATE XXXVIII.

Borderings. May be used around windows, architraves of doors, or near the tops of walls, close to the ceilings where there is no cornice. The two upper are pure Greek in style.

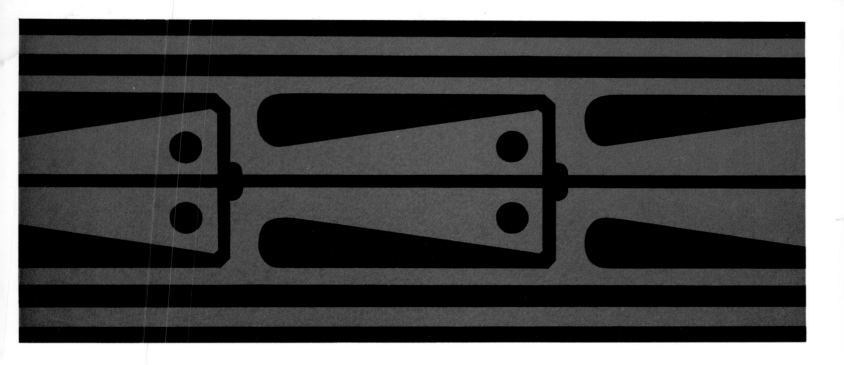

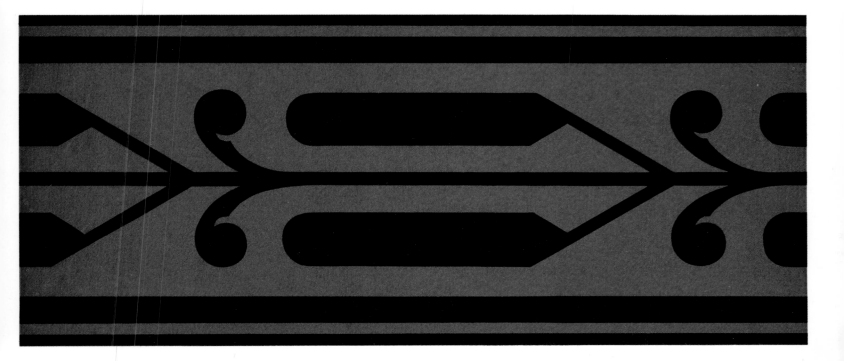

Published by CASSELL, PETTER & GALPIN.

Studies in Design—Plate XXXVIII.

PLATE XXXIX.

Two wall-patterns. That in which the black is introduced would look well with gold used instead of the cream.

Published by CASSELL, PETTER & GALPIN.

STUDIES IN DESIGN—PLATE XXXIX.

PLATE XL.

Ornament treated in two ways. Suitable for centre of panel of door, &c.; or may be brought together as an "all-over" pattern for a wall.

Published by CASSELL, PETTER & GALPIN.

Studies in Design—Plate XL.

PLATE XLI.

Corner ornament for ceiling; to fall within half an inch of cornice. Looks well on cream-ground. Key ornament for centre of side of ceiling. Ornament in left-hand corner is for a cornice enrichment (the coving).

A. Goater. Litho. Nottm.

STUDIES IN DESIGN—PLATE XLI.

Published by CASSELL, PETTER & GALPIN

PLATE XLII:

Ornament for dado, or for wall.

STUDIES IN DESIGN—PLATE XLII.

PLATE XLIII.

Ornament intended to be painted on a ceiling. Style, free Gothic.

DR. DRESSER, INV.

A. GOATER, LITHO. NOTTM.

Published by CASSELL, PETTER & GALPIN.

STUDIES IN DESIGN—PLATE XLIII.

PLATE XLIV.

" All-over ' ornament for a ceiling.

A. Goater, Litho. Nottm.

Published by CASSELL, PETTER & GALPIN.

Studies in Design—Plate XLIV.

PLATE XLV.

Ornaments for panels or dadoes.

Dr. Dresser, Inv.

Published by CASSELL, PETTER & GALPIN.

STUDIES IN DESIGN—PLATE XLV.

A. GOATER, LITHO. NOTTM.

PLATE XLVI.

Grotesques, being part of a dado-rail. This could scarcely be used if simply repeated, but should be intermixed with other creatures designed in the same spirit. Gothic.

DR DRESSER. INV

A. GOATER. LITHO NOTTM

Published by CASSELL, PETTER & GALPIN

STUDIES IN DESIGN—PLATE XLVI.

PLATE XLVII.

Ornaments for the centres of panels of doors, &c. That at the right forms a hideous, grotesque face.

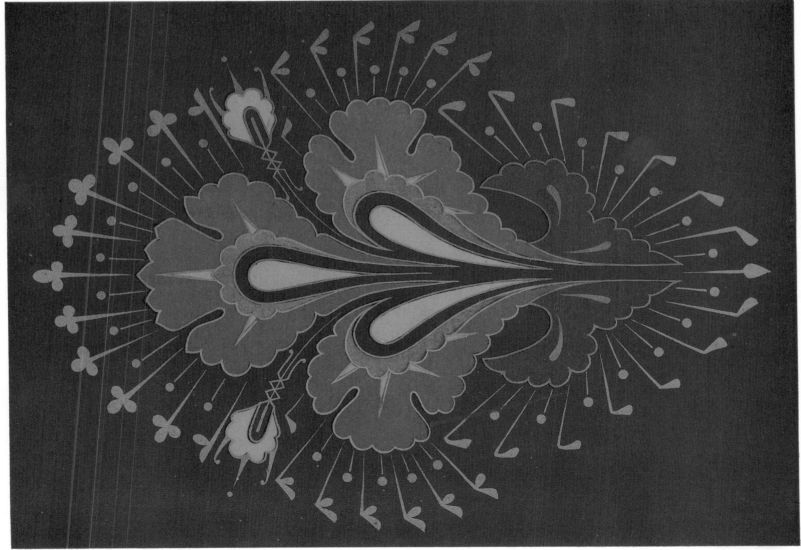

DR. DRESSER, INV.

A. GOATER, LITHO. NOTTM.

Published by CASSELL, PETTER & GALPIN.

STUDIES IN DESIGN—PLATE XLVII.

PLATE XLVIII.

Dado-rails, or frieze ornaments. Style, Arabian. As drawn they are rather small for both purposes, even if the room in which they are used is not large.

Studies in Design—Plate XLVIII.

PLATE XLIX.

Decoration for ceiling.

Published by CASSELL, PETTER & GALPIN.

STUDIES IN DESIGN—PLATE XLIX.

PLATE L.

Two decorations for ceilings.   In repetition, the ornaments would have to be brought near together.

DR. DRESSER, INV.

A. GOATER, LITHO. NOTTM.

Published by CASSELL, PETTER & GALPIN

STUDIES IN DESIGN—PLATE L.

PLATE LI.

Ornament adapted for a wall or dado pattern. Style, Mediæval.

A. GOATER. LITHO. NOTTM.

STUDIES IN DESIGN—PLATE LI.

Published by CASSELL, PETTER & GALPIN

PLATE LII.

Ornament suited for the centre of a panel.

Dr. Dresser, Inv.

Published by CASSELL, PETTER & GALPIN.

Studies in Design—Plate LII.

PLATE LIII.

Ornaments for wall paneling.   Style, free Mediæval.

Published by CASSELL, PETTER & GALPIN. STUDIES IN DESIGN—PLATE LIII.

PLATE LIV.

Ornaments to be used as "powderings" on walls.

DR. DRESSER, INV.

A. GOATER, LITHO. NOTTM.

Published by CASSELL, PETTER & GALPIN.

STUDIES IN DESIGN—PLATE LIV.

PLATE LV.

Ornament for the centre of a small ceiling. This ornament might be repeated over a large ceiling, or would form the centre for a wall panel.

STUDIES IN DESIGN—PLATE LV.

PLATE LVI.

Frieze. To be used around the upper part of the wall of a high room.

DR. DRESSER, INV.

A. GOATER, LITHO. NOTTM.

Published by CASSELL, PETTER & GALPIN.

STUDIES IN DESIGN—PLATE LVI.

PLATE LVII.

Ornaments suited for friezes of small rooms of medium height, or for dado borderings.   Style, Gothic.

Published by CASSELL, PETTER & GALPIN STUDIES IN DESIGN—PLATE LVII.

PLATE LVIII.

Ornament suitable for the decoration of a dado.

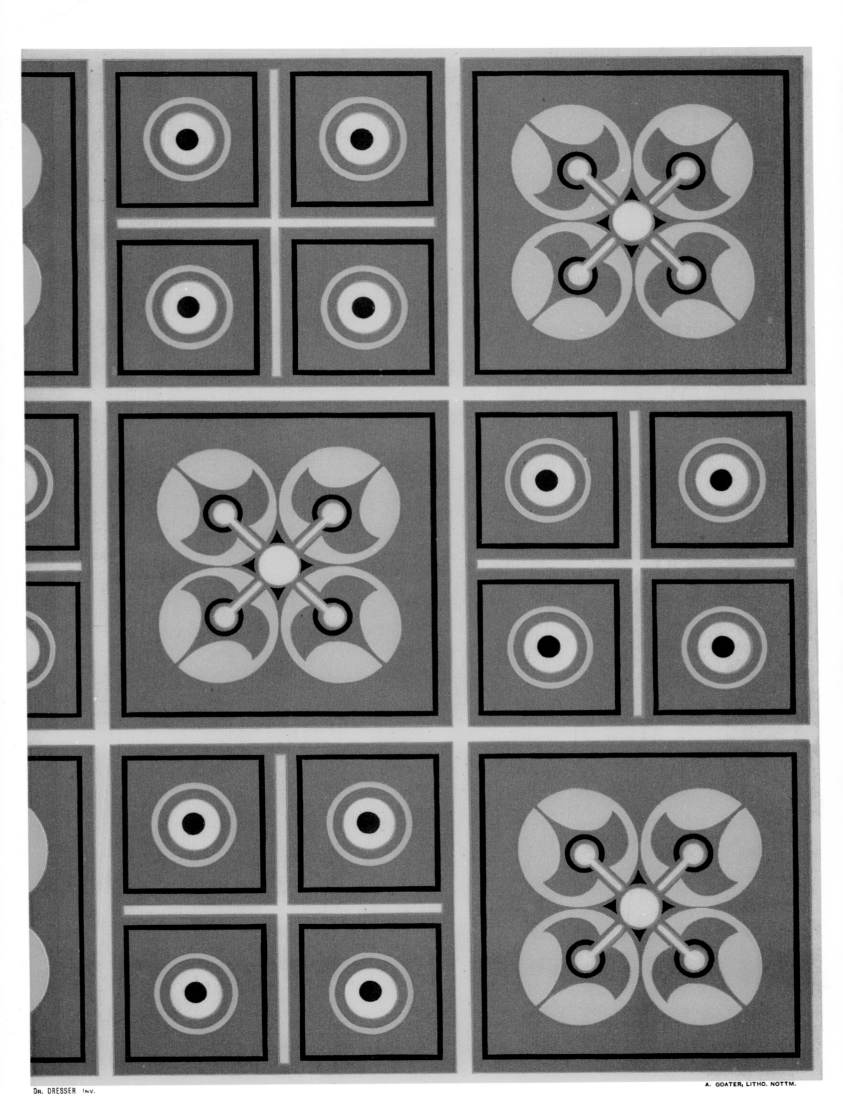

A. GOATER, LITHO. NOTTM.

Published by CASSELL, PETTER & GALPIN.

STUDIES IN DESIGN—PLATE LVIII.

PLATE LIX.

"Powderings," to be dispersed over dadoes or walls.

DR. DRESSER, INV.

A. GOATER, LITHO. NOTTM.

Published by CASSELL, PETTER & GALPIN. STUDIES IN DESIGN—PLATE LIX.

PLATE LX.

Ornament suited for the ornamentation of a passage ceiling.

Dr. DRESSER, Inv

A. GOATER, LITHO. NOTTM.

Published by CASSELL, PETTER & GALPIN.

STUDIES IN DESIGN—PLATE LX.